Forgetting What Lies Behind:

A 31 Day Journey to Freedom

Cindy Holman

To the Refuge Tribe and the CCF Sozo Team for your patience, prayers, and support, as I learned to walk these things out. You have touched me with God's kindness and I will never be the same.

I would like to extend a special thanks to Becky, Christina, and Ellen for your continual prayers. You each find ways to challenge me to rise higher, helping me to believe who God says I am. I am so grateful for you!

Contents

Introduction *6*

1. Cleansing...*10*

2. Forgiveness *13*

3. More on Forgiveness..............................*16*

4. Judgment *19*

5. Judging Yourself *22*

6. Judging Leaders....................................*25*

7. Rich in Mercy..*28*

8. His Yoke is Easy *31*

9. Expectations...*34*

10. Lies *37*

11. Disappointment with Others..................*40*

12. Disappointment with Ourselves *43*

13. Disappointment with Life......................*46*

14. Nothing Can Separate Us from Love......*49*

15. Generational Sins *52*

16. Personal Sin.......................................*55*

17. Vows *58*

18. Idols...*61*

19. Fear of Man...*64*

20. Control *67*

21. A Royal Priesthood, A Holy Nation 70

22. Anger 73

23. Shame 76

24. Reclaiming Your Voice 79

25. Playing it Safe...82

26. Memorials 85

27. The Desires of Your Heart 89

28. Good News 92

29. Maintaining Freedom 95

30. Thanksgiving 98

31. Vision 100

Introduction

Ritchie loved to play with Legos. Any time that he got a chance to choose a center, Ritchie would make a beeline to the Lego bins. As a five-year-old, still learning to share, he had several pieces that he would find and hold on to as soon as he could. He guarded them like treasures and always built the most magnificent creations with them. The other students agreed that Ritchie had mastered the art of building with Legos, and they knew that there would be a battle if they tried to get him to share.

One day the teacher brought out a new science center. She had several interesting rocks and leaves, along with big magnifying glasses. She told the students that they could look at the things on the science table, or they could take the magnifying glasses and explore the room. This idea caught Ritchie's interest. He loved to see how things were put together, and noticed that the other students did not seem very interested in the new activity. Ritchie was itching to go check it out, but he was reluctant to leave his spot with the Legos. Quietly, he gathered up his very favorite Lego pieces and carried them with him to the science area. When he got there, there was one magnifying glass left. As Ritchie reached down to pick it up he found himself with a dilemma. With his hands full of Legos, he could not pick it up. The teacher, who had been watching to see what he would do, said, "Ritchie, you have to let go of the Legos in order to try something new."

This is a familiar place for many of us. We find something that we are good at and we work and work until we master that area of our life. We present our accomplishments before the Lord and His people, and everyone says it is good. But then the Lord begins to prompt us towards something new. He encourages us to dream with Him, and we feel that tug to move forward. But, like Ritchie, before we can step into the new we must let go of a few things.

In Philippians 3:4-6, Paul gives a list of his accomplishments. He had attained the highest levels of religious status in his culture, and in our day he would definitely have been celebrity in the Church. Following his conversion, Paul is known for taking the Gospel to the Gentiles. But as an older man, assumed to be in prison at the time, Paul tells the Philippians that there is still more. In Philippians 3:12-14 he states:

[12] Not that I have already attained, or am already perfected; but I press on, that I may lay hold of that for which Christ Jesus has also laid hold of me. [13] Brethren, I do not count myself to have apprehended; but one thing I do, forgetting those things which are behind and reaching forward to those things which are ahead, [14] I press toward the goal for the prize of the upward call of God in Christ Jesus. (NKJV)

Paul passionately illustrated that he was constantly striving to accomplish all that Jesus had for him, and for him to do that he had to let some things go. You may find yourself in a similar position.

This book is for those who are in a position to move forward, yet have a few things that seem to be getting in the way. Whether you are searching to overcome obstacles that you cannot seem to identify, or just wanting to clean up a few areas of your life, it is my hope that you see some positive changes happening in your life as you read and work through each day. Keep in mind that this book does not have to be read as a traditional daily devotional. You may find you need to stay on a particular subject longer than the others, and some subjects may not apply to you. It can also be used in a small group setting, where you read a few days per week and discuss your thoughts and experiences before praying for one another. You may notice that some of the scenarios I use seem familiar, but be assured that all my examples have been altered to protect those who inspired them.

If you need further support...

On a practical note, there are circumstances that you may find yourself in that require more than a book to overcome. For example, if you are experiencing extreme emotions like fear depression, demonic manifestations, or if you have a background that includes severe traumatic events, then you will need to find people to walk with you as you seek healing. I am confident that the cross and resurrection of Jesus Christ is more than enough to overcome any strongholds. He loves you and wants your freedom and healing more than you do! But the Lord set it up so that we all need each other. The Church is a called a Body for good reason! I encourage you to find a safe environment with caring people to guide you as you seek the Lord's help. There have been, and continue to be, times in my own life where I have sought out such assistance. There is no shame in needing the Church to be the Church for you! If you are a part of a strong church or fellowship, find out what kind of ministries they offer. If you need something further, the following websites will connect you to some ministries that have had a positive influence in my life:

Bethel Sozo - http://bethelsozo.com

International Association of Healing Rooms –
http://healingrooms.com

Restoring the Foundations -
http://restoringthefoundations.org

For more information visit my website at:
www.cindyholman.faith

1. Cleansing

Picture a shepherd down on his knees, cleaning a sheep's hooves. He picks up each hoof and trims it. Then he cleans out the inside of the bottom of the hooves, removing pebbles that cause bruises. Last, he cleans away the mold and disease that have begun to cling to the hooves.

This picture represents the work that the Good Shepherd needs to do from time to time to keep his sheep healthy. The hoof, much like fingernails, is a covering, a form of protection that is useful in many ways. But when they grow too long they get in the way and can become a hindrance to walking. In a similar way, we sometimes outgrow our old coverings, ways of thinking, and defenses. We need Him to come in and trim off the old. The little pebbles that get into our walk and cause us to limp represent offenses and judgments that we hold on to as we go along the way. If we do not allow Him to remove them, they can eventually cripple us. Finally, the mold and disease on the hooves represent the effects of living in a fallen world. As we are part of the sea of humanity, some of it may attach itself to us. That is why we occasionally need Him to come and 'disinfect' us, and reset our ways of thinking.

When we think about serving Jesus, we may dream of being the next Billy Graham, or Mother Theresa. We want to go out and change our world! But we do not often think about the mundane part of the call, the cleansing and the grooming. Esther was called to save her whole nation. Yet, before she ever met the king she went through a whole year of purification. For six months, she was covered with myrrh, which was used to kill parasites, cure halitosis, decrease inflammation, calm the nerves, and many other things. Then, for six months she was covered with perfumes. In Genesis 41:14, Joseph also had to go through cleansing before he was brought to Pharaoh:

14 Then Pharaoh sent and called Joseph, and they brought him quickly out of the dungeon; and he shaved, changed his clothing, and came to Pharaoh. (NKJV)

Joseph had gained favor and had as good of a position as one could have living in the dungeon. But he still had to shave off his beard, the old growth, much like the trimming of the sheep's hooves. He also took off his prison clothes and put on clean ones. Joseph had no idea that he was about to become Pharaoh's right hand man, but you can be sure that he was glad to have cleaned himself up first! It is doubtful that Pharaoh would have had such favor towards him if he had not.

Just like Esther and Joseph, we all have times of preparation. There are things that need to be scrubbed away, trimmed, or disinfected. We need to exchange our old, worn out clothing for new, clean garments that are appropriate for the next season. Like Joseph, we never know who we will find ourselves standing before. Who knows, maybe we have come 'for such a time as this'! As we begin this journey, let's invite God to be in the very center of it. Then, take some time to write down some of the changes that you are hoping to see within yourself.

Prayer:

Father, thank you for loving me enough to clean me up from time to time. I invite you to walk alongside me as I go through this process of purification and preparation. I ask that you would search my heart and show me the things that you want to shift, or change altogether. Thank you, in Jesus' Name. Amen.

Changes I would like to see....

_____

_____

_____

_____

_____

_____

_____

_____

_____

_____

_____

_____

_____

_____

_____

_____

_____

_____

2. Forgiveness

[21] Then Peter came and said to Him, "Lord, how often shall my brother sin against me and I forgive him? Up to seven times?" [22] Jesus said to him, "I do not say to you, up to seven times, but up to seventy times seven. [23] "For this reason the kingdom of heaven may be compared to a king who wished to settle accounts with his slaves. [24] When he had begun to settle them, one who owed him ten thousand talents was brought to him. [25] But since he did not have the means to repay, his lord commanded him to be sold, along with his wife and children and all that he had, and repayment to be made. [26] So the slave fell to the ground and prostrated himself before him, saying, 'Have patience with me and I will repay you everything.' [27] And the lord of that slave felt compassion and released him and forgave him the debt. [28] But that slave went out and found one of his fellow slaves who owed him a hundred denarii; and he seized him and began to choke him, saying, 'Pay back what you owe.' [29] So his fellow slave fell to the ground and began to plead with him, saying, 'Have patience with me and I will repay you.' [30] But he was unwilling and went and threw him in prison until he should pay back what was owed. [31] So when his fellow slaves saw what had happened, they were deeply grieved and came and reported to their lord all that had happened. [32] Then summoning him, his lord said to him, 'You wicked slave, I forgave you all that debt because you pleaded with me. [33] Should you not also have had mercy on your fellow slave, in the same way that I had mercy on you?' [34] And his lord, moved with anger, handed him over to the torturers until he should repay all that was owed him. [35] My heavenly Father will also do the same to you, if each of you does not forgive his brother from your heart." Matthew 18:21-35 (NASB)

I remember reading this passage when I was in Jr. High School. I found it confusing that Jesus said if we didn't forgive we would be given over to tormentors. That did not sound like the Jesus I had put all my trust in! But as the years have gone by, I have seen over and over the devastation that living with unforgiveness has brought, both in my own life and in the lives of others. For me, the key to getting free from bitterness, anger, and pain, was in forgiving those who had hurt me.

Forgiveness is one of the key issues in growing and moving forward in the Christian life. Much like the principle of sowing and reaping, the Lord makes it very clear that we are responsible for the choices we make in this area. It is simple - if we forgive we will be able to walk away from it, but if we do not forgive we will live in torment. What does torment look like? Consider for a moment a time in your life when someone did something to you that stuck with you. When you went home you were still thinking about it. You may have had a conversation with that person in your mind, telling them how you really felt about them. You may even have told everyone you know what they did to you and how awful you thought they were. Then you felt convicted. The Holy Spirit began to remind you what the Bible says about forgiveness and gossip, and you repented and decided not to do it again. But soon you found yourself mulling over the situation in your mind again and again. Sound familiar? The enemy was tormenting your mind with thoughts about the incident, and every time you agreed with those thoughts instead of choosing forgiveness you were agreeing with the enemy. We have all done it, and we will all have daily opportunities to choose who to listen to in the future. But the amazing kindness of our God is that He provides a way out. If we will come to Him as a loving Father and repent, talk to Him about changing your mind and choosing to be like Him, and then forgive, He will forgive us and restore our peace.

Prayer:

Father, thank you for loving me so much that you have forgiven me for all the ways I have wronged you and others. I ask that you would help me to be more like you by forgiving the people who have hurt me. I ask that you would bring to my mind the names of people that I need to forgive, and what they did that I am holding on to. As I let them go, Father, I ask that you would fill me with your love and help me to walk in mercy. Thank you, in Jesus' Name. Amen.

3. More on Forgiveness

Several years ago, a lady named Beth joined a women's group at her church. At first she enjoyed going there, but as time went on, the leaders of that group decided that they needed to 'fix' her. They would meet with her, tell her what was wrong with her, and 'pray' for her. One day they met with her at a restaurant. As they were doing what they called 'ministry', one of the women stood up, leaned over her, thumped her on the head, and said, "You stink!" This incident deeply hurt Beth's feelings and had a lasting impact on my her. Years later, she would be catching up with her friends, and like clockwork, she would bring up that memory. They had commiserated over it many times. Finally, one day her friends gently pointed out that while she was still being tormented by the memory, those people probably never thought of that moment again. They reminded her of the passage where Jesus talked about forgiveness in Matthew 18. At that point Beth was ready to be free of the incident. She chose to forgive the ladies, and found herself free of the repetitive thoughts and anguish she had suffered with for so many years!

I have found that there are many ways that people look at forgiveness. I have talked with people who could not see themselves ever forgiving because of the severity of the offense they suffered, and I have talked to those who refuse to admit that there is anything that needs to be forgiven, even when there has been a great offense. In between those two extremes I have found that many of us have created a kind of scale in our minds about which things are forgivable and which things are just too heinous to overlook. We stand in judgment over others who have overstepped our 'line', and when we are the victims of their behavior we feel vindicated in partnering with hatred towards them. But what we often fail to see is the trap that we have created for ourselves. Now please let me be clear, I am not saying that what the offenders did was not horrible. I know that there are many who have been severely traumatized, stolen from, and have suffered abuses of all kinds. The key here is not in deciding what was right or wrong, but rather who is sitting on the Seat of Judgment. When I was young, I was taught that comparing the levels of people's goodness was like a long jump competition across the Grand Canyon. When I jump, my goodness, or lack of sin, might take me a several feet, but when someone with a lot of sin jumps they may just go a few inches. Either way, we fall into the Grand Canyon. None of us is good enough to get all the way across. Every person's sin was so great that it cost Jesus everything. When we compare our sins to each other's, it's easy to form a rating scale. But when we focus on how much debt He has forgiven us, it becomes clear that He alone has earned the right to make any judgment call. In asking us to forgive, He is asking us to let Him sit in His rightful place.

Sometimes we have memories where we were so hurt that forgiveness seems impossible. For some of you, there may be one or two difficult areas that you are struggling to let go. The words, "But you don't know what they did!" keep rising within you. If this is the case, you might need to get extra help, as I mentioned in the

17

introduction. I encourage you to find someone to pray with you in person. (See pages 8-9 for more details.)

Take a moment to ask the Lord to show you anyone that you still need to forgive. It is time to get free from the pain that unforgiveness has over you, and let Jesus be the one on the judgment seat!

Prayer:

Jesus, thank you for forgiving me of more than I can ever imagine. I ask you to help me to forgive the people who have hurt me so badly that I've had a hard time letting go. I bring them and the incidents to You, knowing that what you, a perfect and sinless man, suffered for me was beyond comprehension. I leave them there at the alter with You, and I ask that you would heal the wounds they inflicted upon me. Please take away the pain of the memories and fill me with your peace. Thank you! Amen.

4. Judgment

After spending a couple of days dealing with forgiveness, it is now time to explore the area of judgment in our lives. When we read scriptures on forgiveness, the word translated as *forgiveness* basically referred to a cancelling of a debt. The word *judgment,* on the other hand, refers to forming an opinion, or even declaring an opinion of right or wrong. Matthew 7:1-2 states:

"Judge not, that you be not judged. ² For with what judgment you judge, you will be judged; and with the measure you use, it will be measured back to you. (NKJV)

Picture for a moment, a group of people dressed in pure white running along a path. They are heading into the wind, and as they move forward, one of them makes a critical comment about another to the person next to him. As the words are spoken, they gush forward into the air a couple of feet, and then the wind blows those words right back at the speaker, landing in dark letters written across his shirt. The words are weighty, and the runner must work a little harder to keep up. Every once in a while, that process is repeated. When one of the runners speaks words of judgment, it comes right back onto them, adding to the weight of their load and soiling their appearance. Of course, the ones who do not speak judgment move way out in front of the others, having less weight to carry. It is like that in our lives. We are made in God's image, so when we speak our words are very powerful. Proverbs 18:21a says, "Death and life are in the power of the tongue." (NKJV). We have the choice of speaking life or death into the situations around us. It is the basic concept of sowing and reaping, where we can sow hope and encouragement and those things will come back to us, or we can sow judgment over people, which will in turn also come back upon us.

I went through a season of my life where it felt like everything that I attempted to do fell flat. I put in long hours, and I studied hard. I did my best to live without unforgiveness, and I was hitting all the basics – reading the Bible, prayer, fellowship, worship… But for some reason the people around me always got promoted or recognized over me. After a while, the frustration of my circumstances drove me to my knees, seeking an answer. It was in that place of humility that I saw my need to change my attitude. I had been standing in judgment over some people in my life, and I was reaping the consequences of those judgments. I began to repent and ask the Lord to show me how He saw those people and to fill me with His love for them, and then my heart began to change.

If the measure we use for someone else will be used to measure us, it would be a good idea to consider what measure we are using. For example, when you look at how other people go about their lives, do you have compassion and understanding for their struggle mixed in with your thoughts, or are you frustrated and critical of them? Is there sarcasm or haughtiness? Do you speak with a tone that lets everyone know what you really think? We can ask these questions in every area of our lives.

Take a moment to consider the people and situations in different areas of your life...

- Family
- Workplace
- Church
- Neighbors
- Driving
- Gym

Prayer:

Father, thank you for having so much patience with me. You have poured out your mercy when I deserved only judgment from you. I repent, or change my attitude towards the people that I have stood in judgment over. (Name them individually.) I ask you to help me to make a real change in the way I respond towards those who don't think or act the way I do. Thank you, in Jesus' Name. Amen.

5. Judging Yourself

There was once a young man who loved to play soccer. He played soccer every time he got a chance, and he was good at it. One day he was on his way to meet with a group of friends to play a game, when his father asked him to stay home and help get down some boxes from the attic. The boy was not to be bothered with menial household chores when there was fun to be had, so he put off his dad and went on his way. About halfway through the game, one of his sisters came running up to the field, calling for the young man. She told him that his dad had fallen while trying to bring down the boxes and had broken his leg. For some time, the young man had to spend his extra time taking care of the family while his dad recovered. He got a part time job and helped his mother around the house. Even after his dad had recovered, he continued to be a very responsible son. But he never went back to playing soccer. When his friends asked him why, he would just shake his head and look off into the distance. You see, the young man was so filled with shame and guilt over his behavior that day, he was convinced that he did not deserve to have fun or be childlike ever again.

Sometimes there are areas of our lives where we are holding ourselves accountable for something that happened a long time ago. Whether it is something that we in fact did, or something that we perceive about ourselves, we stand in judgment against ourselves and limit what we allow ourselves to receive. For some people this can be based on a serious incident, like a car accident or tragedy of some kind. For others, it can be that they feel responsible for family issues like their parent's divorce, or maybe their own. Many people judge themselves because they believe words that other people have spoken over them, usually from a parent, teacher, or authority figure. Often the self-judgment can be partnered with shame, guilt, rejection, self-pity, and self-hatred, trapping the person inside a miserable prison that can cause depression and sometimes illness. If you are dealing with deep depression or worse, please get help. (See pages 8-9 for more details.)

So, what can we do if we realize that we have this kind of problem in our life? You start by forgiving yourself. You come out of agreement with the judgments that you or others have put over you and receive forgiveness. If you say that your sin is too great to be forgiven, you deny the work of Jesus on the cross and say His sacrifice wasn't good enough for you. So, dare to come out of agreement with shame and guilt and the rest, and lay them all down at the foot of the cross. Sometimes it helps to picture yourself doing just that. Remember that 1 John 1:9 says:

[9] If we confess our sins, He is faithful and just to forgive us *our* sins and to cleanse us from all unrighteousness. (NKJV)

Take time to quiet yourself and ask the Lord to show you any area of your life where you need to 'take yourself off the hook'. Are there any areas of your life where your own expectations of yourself are greater than His? As He reveals things to you, forgive yourself and come out of agreement with the judgments that you have walked under. Ask Him to show you how to be childlike again, because His yoke is easy and His burden is light!

Prayer:

Father, thank you for the love and mercy that you lavish over me. You do not stand over me in judgment for sin, but you see me clean because of the Blood of Jesus that covers me. I choose to forgive myself today, and I come out of agreement with shame, guilt, rejection, self-pity, self-hatred, and anything else that I have agreed with. I ask you to help me to change my attitude towards myself and to love myself the way you do. Thank you, in Jesus' Name. Amen.

6. Judging Leaders

[13] For judgment *will be* merciless to one who has shown no mercy; mercy triumphs over judgment. James 2:13 (NASB)

Here is another opportunity to let mercy triumph! There are a few more areas of judgment that you might not have considered.

Your government - Whether you approve of the officials who are currently governing your country or not, it is most probable that there have been some issues that you feel strongly about. Compounded by a media that has learned the power of persuasion, and social media, opinions and judgments about leaders and situations are unavoidable. Consequently, instead of praying for these leaders in a positive and life-giving way, you may find yourself tempted to pray with an attitude about them - if you pray for them at all. But if "life and death are in the power of the tongue," as we read yesterday, then we should be praying for life and godliness to be restored, not devastation or destruction.

Celebrities, athletes, or persons of interest – Most people know the familiar story of the married actor who has an affair and ends up leaving his wife for a new love interest. The genders may be switched, but it happens all too often. Sometimes celebrities get caught doing something illegal or embarrassing, and if it is a slow news day their private failures will be plastered all over the media, talked about on late night shows, and social media will have them tried and sentenced within a few minutes. If you have ever been caught up in this kind of frenzy, then you probably participated in judgment, especially if you felt disappointed.

People who are different than you – We know that racism is a catalyst for judgement and accusation, and it comes from all sides. We need to take a very serious and prayerful look at the way we view people groups. If we ask the Lord to show us our hearts in this area, He will show us where we need to change. He will also provide the way for us to make those changes. The Lord said in Matthew 5:44 that we should love our enemies and pray for those who persecute us. We may not feel persecuted here in the Western church, but consider people who support abortion, gay rights, socialism, gambling, etc. Consider what kinds of feelings do these words stir within you: yoga, Harry Potter, tattoos, marijuana, perpetrator, trans-gender. As citizens of heaven, our ministry is that of reconciliation, not judgment. (2 Corinthians 5:18) Isn't the person who has been deceived just as much a victim of the enemy? I believe there is a place for standing up for what we believe in, for voting, for educating people on the consequences of sin in their lives, and for standing up for justice. But let's remember who the battle is really with and let go of judgment towards the people or groups that we see as enemies. Ephesians 6:12 states:

[12] For our struggle is not against flesh and blood, but against the rulers, against the powers, against the world forces of this darkness, against the spiritual forces of wickedness in the heavenly places. (NASB)

I find that when I remind myself of this truth it is much easier to step out of judgment and love the people, even though I find their behavior difficult. This is when the truth that Jesus was resurrected with the keys to death, hell, and the grave is so comforting. He has full authority over the enemy, so you can come to Him knowing that He has the keys you need to overcome as well, all the while loving the people He loves.

Prayer:

Father, thank you that your mercy has triumphed over the judgment that I deserve. Thank you for showing me areas of my life where I have been standing in judgment over people or people groups. I repent, or change my attitude towards the people that I have stood in judgment over. (Name them.) I ask you to help me to make a real change in the way I think about those who don't think or act the way I do. Thank you, in Jesus' Name. Amen.

7. Rich in Mercy

[4] But God, being rich in mercy, because of His great love with which He loved us, [5] even when we were dead in our transgressions, made us alive together with Christ (by grace you have been saved), [6] and raised us up with Him, and seated us with Him in the heavenly places in Christ Jesus, [7] so that in the ages to come He might show the surpassing riches of His grace in kindness toward us in Christ Jesus. [8] For by grace you have been saved through faith; and that not of yourselves, it is the gift of God; [9] not as a result of works, so that no one may boast. [10] For we are His workmanship, created in Christ Jesus for good works, which God prepared beforehand so that we would walk in them. Ephesians 2:4-10. (NASB)

I started reading the Bible when I was in Jr. High School, and I read this passage many times. But it took decades before I really believed what it said. I always had something driving me to do the right thing. The people around me thought I was very spiritual. I set a standard that was extremely high and they couldn't even attempt to live up to it. But the truth was that I only felt lovable when I was good. I somehow got the idea that my value came from what I did. I was blessed with a loving and supportive family who did their best to help me past this. But religious thinking can be very difficult to overcome. Over the years I had some breakthrough because I was seeking after Jesus with all my heart. I would cling to the Scriptures and find comfort in them, but I always had doubts.

After years and years of trying to be good enough I got very discouraged and basically gave myself over to bitterness. One evening I found myself in a prayer meeting that I had not even intended to go to. As I sat there listening, a young man got on the microphone and said, "God loves you and He's in a good mood." For some reason those words were like an arrow to my heart. The thought that God was not austere, that he was not frustrated with my sin, was like a lightbulb in my soul. I was so affected that I took a bold step that night and dared to believe that it might be true. As I continued to attend that prayer house their message was always the same, and I found myself healing on the inside. I was challenged to firmly believe this passage in Ephesians, and as I took those steps of faith my sense of value began to change.

Many people in the world struggle with the same idea of needing to be good enough. It is hard to embrace the truth that Jesus died for all your sins, including your future ones. We are so grateful for His forgiveness that it can be devastating to realize that we have let Him down yet again. But as stated above, we are saved by having faith in God's grace and His goodness, not by working hard enough to please Him.

Whether this passage in Ephesians is new and challenging for you, or familiar like an old friend, today is a good day to stop and consciously ponder the implications of what it means to your life in Christ. I challenge you to read through it slowly, spend time on each phrase, and savor the love that God has poured out over you. I dare you to believe that when you see the words 'we' and 'us' that you are included. In fact, you may want to read it aloud and substitute your own name in place of those words. Then take a moment to write down the truth about yourself and how God sees you.

Prayer:

Father, thank you for your great mercy and grace towards me. Thank you for loving me before I cleaned myself up, so that our relationship is not based on me trying to be good enough, but rather on what Jesus did for me by dying on the cross. Thank you that you have raised me up to be seated with you. I ask that you will show me the things that you have prepared me to do in this world, as an expression of how much I love you. In Jesus' Name, amen.

The truth about who I am and how God sees me:

_____

_____

_____

_____

_____

_____

_____

_____

_____

8. His Yoke is Easy

Picture a group of young children wearing long heavy oversized woolen coats trudging along the beach on a warm summer's day. Along comes a semi-truck with a light blue cab and a white trailer barreling down to the end of the road. The truck driver, wearing a black cap with a lightning bolt on the front covering his long curly dark hair, climbs down from the cab. The children cautiously gather near and a high-pitched voice shouts out, "What's in the truck?" With a toothy grin the truck driver answers, "It's a truckload of 'My yoke is easy and my burden is light!'" Then he goes around the truck and opens the back. The children look at each other like this guy is crazy, but they go around the back, too, as curiosity gets the best of them. They see boxes in the truck and the driver begins to open them. To their delight he pulls out lightweight, golden, super hero-like capes. With wide eyes, one of the children asks, "What do you want for one of those?" The driver smiles and says, "You must give me that heavy coat you are wearing." Happily, they quickly exchange their heavy coats for the capes, laughing and chattering as they do so. Once they are finished, the children feel like they can accomplish anything, so they all run down to the water's edge to practice walking on water. Some start to get the hang of it and some still sink to the ground, but they all know that they can accomplish great things if they put their minds to it.

Sometimes in the middle of everyday life we get caught up in all that needs to be done, and we start to take on burdens that wear us out. This world is filled with a myriad of pressures to be this and do that, we have family issues and financial demands, and so much more. Before we know it, life feels heavy and burdensome, and worry and fear threaten to move in. It is at that point that the Lord's words in Matthew 11:28-30 provide a plan:

28 "Come to Me, all who are weary and heavy-laden, and I will give you rest. 29 Take My yoke upon you and learn from Me, for I am gentle and humble in heart, and you will find rest for your souls. 30 For My yoke is easy and My burden is light." Matt 11:28-30. (NASB)

This is an invitation by Jesus, the King of Kings, to partner with Him and let Him carry the brunt of your load. You will need to trust Him with some things, like your family, your future, and your hopes and dreams. But you will find that He is trustworthy. He paid his taxes with money He found in the mouth of a fish, so He can find a way to help you with your finances. He knows how to heal families, He can make a way where there is no way, and His hopes for you are even greater than your own. It may take some time, but if you continue to find your rest in Him and learn from Him, you will live in peace.

Just like those kids on the beach, now is a great time to take off your heavy burdens and exchange them for Jesus' covering. Take a few moments to reflect over different areas of your life and ask the Lord to point out any area where you are carrying more than He has asked you to carry. These burdens may be things that circumstances or others have put on you, or responsibilities that you have taken on yourself. Once you recognize something, ask Jesus what it would look like to let Him have it. Then give it to Him. It may help to write it down so you can come back and remind yourself to let Him keep it.

Prayer:

Jesus, thank you for being my burden-bearer! I ask that you would open my eyes to see where I have taken on burdens that you did not ask me to carry, and show me how to give them back to you. Thank you that you are so gentle and kind. Please teach me how to rest in you! In Your Name, amen.

Burdens that I am giving to Jesus:

_____

_____

_____

_____

_____

_____

_____

_____

_____

_____

_____

_____

9. Expectations

I love families. God created a beautiful picture of what our relationship of love with Him is supposed to look like, by putting us in families. Unfortunately, our family relationships are not perfect. Even the best parents with the highest intentions will make mistakes along the way. This reinforces our need to bring God into our relationships, because if we do they will be much better. But even then, most people still walk away with some areas of dysfunction. One of these areas is expectations.

The scene is not unfamiliar. A young man is being groomed to take over the family business when a young woman comes into his life and challenges him to follow his dreams. He finally finds the courage to tell his father that he wants to be an artist, and in the end his dad sees how important it is to him and gives his blessing. That is easy enough when you live in a movie or on the pages of a book. But for some people there has been no way of escape from what is expected. Whether it is because of circumstances, or the element of showing respect for the family, you may find yourself trapped in a cycle of living up to other people's expectations.

On the flip side, the expectation of some families is that of never measuring up. I know of people whose parents called them stupid, or said they would never amount to anything. Maybe a teacher or another authority figure told you that you don't have what it takes to live your dreams. Their opinions echoed inside your mind until you found yourself coming into agreement with them.

In Luke 19:1-10, Jesus calls out to a tax collector names Zacchaeus. Zacchaeus was a short man who earned his living collecting money from the people for the Romans, their oppressors. When Jesus talked to him, the people around him began to grumble, indicating that they all knew who he was. He was a rejected bad boy and they already had made their judgments about him. But there was a miracle about to happen that day. When Jesus let Zacchaeus know that he saw him and invited him into relationship, the man was changed. Suddenly, he was generous and repentant. Jesus went to Zacchaeus' house for dinner that night, despite what anyone else thought of him. He said that his purpose was to seek out and save those who are lost.

Whether you fit within one of these scenarios or not, it is likely that there have been some expectations put on your life. They may be big things, or they may just be little things that you have put upon yourself. Either way, they can become heavy burdens, and sometimes they can block us from walking in the fullness of what God has for our lives.

As we come to a time of asking Jesus to show us the places in our lives where we are trying to live up to the expectations of others, I encourage you to allow Him access into the depths of your heart. He sees you. He knows all about you and loves you to the point of death anyway. He is your best friend. It doesn't matter what anybody else thinks of you, He is completely for you. Ask

Him to show you if there are any adjustments that you need to make in this area of your life, and write down any goals that come to mind.

Prayer:

Jesus, thank you for seeing the real me. You know my thoughts, my hopes, and the desires of my heart. I ask that you would open my eyes to see where I have been trying to live up to the expectations of others, and show me what your expectations are of me. Please show me if there are any changes that you want me to make, and then show me how to make them. Thank you for believing in me! In Your Name, amen.

Goals:

_____

_____

_____

_____

_____

_____

_____

_____

_____

_____

_____

10. Lies

When I was a little girl, probably about four years old, one of my playmates told me that I couldn't like the color purple because that was her color. As silly as it sounds, I believed her and avoided purple for many years. When I was in my twenties I realized that I really like purple and it flatters me, so now it is one of the main colors in my wardrobe. Obviously, the other little girl was just acting like ninety per cent of little girls in our society. Most of them love purple! But for some reason I held on to that lie and made it a part of my identity.

It is not uncommon for us to find these silly little beliefs in our view of the world. As children, we observed how society worked as we experienced life and sometimes came to wrong conclusions. If there was no one there to help us form realistic ideas, then our perceptions may still be a little off. Of course, some misconceptions, or lies, about ourselves or the world are more harmful than others. Avoiding purple is not a big issue, but thinking of oneself as flawed in some way has the potential to negatively impact life decisions.

When Katherine was a child, her dad longed to have a little boy. Her dad never quite learned how to relate to a girl, so he would ask her to play sports and treated her like a tomboy. Since Katherine loved to be with her dad she embraced this identity. She worked hard to become strong and tough, she shortened her name to Kat, and at some point, forgot to learn what it means to be feminine. As she got older, people around her began to question her sexual identity and she found herself in some uncomfortable situations. Katherine had learned to get validation and love for being boy-like, and she wasn't sure how to be any other way. So, she kept to herself. Then Kat met Jesus. He filled so much of the emptiness in her heart that she felt like a new person. One day, when she was in a prayer session, the Lord brought her to the point of forgiving her dad for wanting a son and not embracing her as a daughter. When she was finished, she was asked to come out of agreement with the lie that demanded she act like a boy. The Lord revealed to her the truth, that she was born to be beautiful girl and that it was okay to act like one. After that Katherine took little steps towards embracing her more feminine side. She made subtle changes to her appearance, tried some movies that evoked emotions, and began going by the name of Katherine. She still loved sports and actions movies, and she never could quite understand the big deal about flowers, but she was much more comfortable in her own skin.

I believe that all of us have some degree of colored lenses that skew our view of reality. The difficult part of it is that they seem reasonable to us, so they can be hard to detect. But we have been blessed with the precious Holy Spirit, who knows how to search our hearts and minds, and bring us into all truth. Let's ask Him to lead us into that truth. Open your heart to see any areas that He might bring to your thoughts, and listen closely. Then break agreement with the lies that you have believed, and dare to ask Him to show you the truth. Sometimes the truth is so good that we have a hard time believing that we are really hearing from God. The way you can test that is through Scripture. Is He saying you can accomplish things? Philippians 4:13 says you can do all things through Christ who gives you strength. Is He saying you are beautiful? Isaiah 61:3 says that He exchanges His beauty for your ashes. I challenge you to believe, write down, and meditate on the truths that He says about you.

Prayer:

Holy Spirit, thank you for guiding me into all truth. You know how to search my heart and my mind and you see all things. I ask that you would open my eyes to see where I have believed lies about myself or about how the world works. I also ask that you would tell me the truth about myself and the world. I ask that you would confirm the things that you are putting in my heart over the next few days, so that I will be sure that I am hearing from you clearly. Thank you! In Jesus' Name, amen.

What does God say about you?

_____

_____

_____

_____

_____

_____

_____

11. Disappointment with Others

They were supposed to be faithful. They were supposed to walk with me through thick and thin. They promised me the moon...and then they failed me. I can understand what went wrong. I can have compassion for their struggle. But I am so disappointed. I just can't put too much hope in them again. It is simply not worth the risk!

How many of us have had those kinds of feelings? We have all had times when we were let down by people we put our confidence in. Whether it was a parent, a friend, a leader, or a spouse, when someone lets us down it wounds us. Our reaction is often to become angry, and sometimes we hold what the person did over their heads. We tell everyone what they did or didn't do, and bring it up every time the issue of trust comes up. Even after we have forgiven the person we can still have a lingering sore spot, and it can be hard to trust again.

Paul dealt with disappointment. When he and Barnabas embarked on their missionary journey they took Barnabas' cousin John, who was also called Mark, with them. During their travels, they got into some trouble and John Mark deserted them. Later, when they were setting out again, Barnabas wanted to take John Mark with them once more. But Paul was so against this that he and Barnabas argued and parted ways, and so Paul continued his journey without Barnabas. Thankfully, Paul got over his disappointment with 'Mark', because later in his life he mentioned that Mark was with him and that the people should welcome him (Colossians 4:10). It was this same John Mark who is believed to have written the book of Mark, one of the four gospels. The truth is that when you are interacting with people, you are going to be disappointed at some point. People are flawed. Even those with the highest of intentions fail from time to time. Remember that in Philippians 3, Paul said that he had not reached perfection yet, but he kept working toward it. So, the first step in dealing with disappointment is to recognize that truth.

On the night He was betrayed, Jesus knew that Peter was going to deny Him - three times! He must have been incredibly disappointed! What was His response? He prayed for Peter and focused on his potential. Jesus did not write Peter off, instead He looked for a way to help Peter grow through the experience, recognizing that Peter's love was true even though his behavior was not. If we want to be like Jesus, we need to learn to see people like He does. This may mean that you need to adjust your own expectations of the other person as they learn and grow. Jesus is the only Perfect One. Keep in mind the kind of grace you would like them to extend to you and do the same for them.

Take a few moments and ask the Holy Spirit to show you any areas of your life where you are struggling with disappointment in people. If you feel an anger rise within you when you think of the circumstances, then you may need to repent and break all agreement with anger. Then take the pain that remains and pour it out to Jesus, leaving it there with Him. He understands your pain because He was also disappointed. Ask Him to heal those areas in your heart and to help you to see the person or people who hurt you through His eyes. Finally, ask Him to give you realistic expectations in your relationships.

Prayer:

Jesus, thank you for looking beyond the times I have failed you, and seeing my potential. You know the ways that people have let me down, and the pain that I have endured because of their actions. I ask that you would help me to let go of the disappointment and the pain, and to see the person or people through your eyes. Help me to remember that you are the only one who never fails. In Your Name, amen!

12. Disappointment with Ourselves

I have always been drawn to music. When I was in college I began writing little songs, and ten years later I wrote an album. I had friends who knew a guy with a studio and I ended up recording it. I had such big dreams at the time. I wanted to reach the world with the gospel and I wanted a different career. But I soon realized that I was lacking in the drive and confidence that it took to work in the music industry. I got criticized a few times, and once all my friends and family had bought my album it all fizzled out. I was disappointed. I had to face a part of myself that was not as good as I had hoped. I didn't turn out to be the person that I thought I was, so I buried music for a while. As I kept on a brave face and tried to hide my discouragement, I found that other things like embarrassment and resentment were trying to hang around as well. I did whatever I could to avoid the people who had been in my life when I was in the recording process. They would ask how my music was going and I would find a way to quickly leave, or, I would laugh at myself and tell them that my dreams had been a little too big. But inside I was in a lot of pain. It was during that process that I changed my view of myself, altering my expectation and hopes, as well. For years, I tried to put restrictions on how I invested in music, but the need to write and sing would just not go away! When I did try to step out again, the slightest hint of rejection would send me back into seclusion and self-pity again. It was a painful and frustrating issue for me for a long time. Finally, one day the Lord highlighted this area when I was in a time of prayer. He pointed out that I was blaming myself in a way that not only dishonored me, but dishonored Him. He gave me the gift of music and I had devoted it to Him. There was a lack of trust. I was assuming that because it had not gone the way I expected, I must have messed it up and disappointed us both. But He was not disappointed in my failure, He was disappointed in my attitude towards myself. He asked me to forgive myself and allow myself the same grace that He had for me. 2 Corinthians 12:9-10 states:

[9] And He has said to me, "My grace is sufficient for you, for power is perfected in weakness." Most gladly, therefore, I will rather boast about my weaknesses, so that the power of Christ may dwell in me.[10] Therefore I am well content with weaknesses, with insults, with distresses, with persecutions, with difficulties, for Christ's sake; for when I am weak, then I am strong. (NASB)

Just like we must accept that other people are flawed, we need to recognize the we will make mistakes along the way. That is the place in our lives that we rejoice in the truth that we are saved by the redemption of the cross and that our goodness has nothing to do with it. We recognize that the Lord still believes in us and His purpose for our life has not been altered. He knows how to make all things work together for good, even our failure.

There are many places in life that we can become disappointed with ourselves. Sometimes we have areas of sin or weakness. In Romans 7, Paul talks about the struggle with our old nature and concludes that it is only with the help of the Holy Spirit that we can overcome sin. Other people struggle with being a good parent or spouse, and have become disappointed with themselves because of the mistakes they have made. Or, maybe like me, they had goals for their lives that they did not accomplish.

Take a few moments to ask the Holy Spirit to show you if there are any areas of your life where you are disappointed with yourself. Then take time to forgive yourself and receive God's grace.

Prayer:

Jesus, thank you that your grace is sufficient for me. You know the ways that I have failed, and the resulting pain that I have suffered. I ask that you would help me to let go of the disappointment and the pain, and to see the myself through your eyes. Show me the ways that I expect more of myself than you do, and help me to walk in your grace. In Your Name, amen!

13. Disappointment with Life

When we were young we dreamed of what our adult life would look like. Many of us expected to have a home and a family, and a job we enjoy going to every day. Little girls dreamed about their knights in shining amour and little boys dreamed about being a superhero or a professional athlete. But the dreams of little children are rarely reflected in the reality that we face as adults, and that can lead to great disappointment. Most of us have experienced that moment in our lives when we realized that things were not going to happen the way we had hoped. Whether it had to do with marriage and family, or our career path, we had to decide in that moment how we were going to deal with it. We had a choice to either give in to despair and hopelessness, or choose to accept the setback and press on towards the plans and purposes of God in our lives while holding on to hope. Proverbs 13:12, states:

Hope deferred makes the heart sick, but desire fulfilled is a tree of life. (NASB)

When we lose hope we can find ourselves in depression and lethargy, and eventually it can lead to illness. It can become a downward spiral that seems to be endless. But there is a way out! When we let go and dare to believe again we will begin to see a light at the end of the tunnel. Jesus has not given up on you and He is waiting for any sign of surrender to Him. If you find yourself in that kind of a dark place where you don't see any way out, you may need people who will gather around you and support you on your journey. (See pages 8-9 for more details.)

When I was younger I became very disappointed with God. I trusted Him to do something I thought I had heard Him promise, even when the people around me thought I was foolish. I was attempting to stand in great faith, and I wouldn't listen to wise counsel. But it did not turn out well for me, and I found myself both humiliated and disappointed. I had a moment where I literally raised my fist to the heavens and told God that He had let me down. My whole faith was on the line and I was finished following Him. I deserved to be forsaken at that point. I deserved to be left alone to my own devices. But that isn't what He did. Every night when I was about to go to sleep I would hear His voice deep inside me saying, "I love you! I love you!" I remember telling Him to be quiet and leave me alone. He would be quiet until the next night, then He would start again, "I love you!" This went on for several months. But how can you stand against that kind of love? I finally gave in and repented. I surrendered my life to Him again and moved forward. Since then I have had many more opportunities to decide if I will trust God or demand my own way. I do not always get what I want, but I have His love. I know beyond a shadow of a doubt that He never gives up on me, which is the foundation for everything else in my life, and I am at peace.

I have people in my life who have suffered great loss, so I know that this can be a difficult subject for some of you. Others may simply need to deal with small areas of dissatisfaction with your life. Either way, it is time to give those disappointments to the Lord and let Him bring healing and comfort into your life. If, like me, you have blamed God for your troubles, you need to realize that you have cut yourself off from the very flow of life and peace that you are searching for. Humble yourself and ask for forgiveness, let Him have it, and let Him love you into a place of healing.

Prayer:

Father, thank you that you keep loving me even when I disappoint you. You know the places in my life where I have been disappointed and disillusioned. You see the places where I have given up on my dreams, even the ones that you have put in my heart. I choose to open my heart up to you again, daring to risk hope once more. I ask you to comfort me in those places of loss and to blanket me again in your love. In Jesus' Name, amen!

14. Nothing Can Separate Us from Love

[28] And we know that God causes all things to work together for good to those who love God, to those who are called according to His purpose. [29] For those whom He foreknew, He also predestined to become conformed to the image of His Son, so that He would be the firstborn among many brethren; [30] and these whom He predestined, He also called; and these whom He called, He also justified; and these whom He justified, He also glorified. [31] What then shall we say to these things? If God is for us, who is against us? [32] He who did not spare His own Son, but delivered Him over for us all, how will He not also with Him freely give us all things? [33] Who will bring a charge against God's elect? God is the one who justifies; [34] who is the one who condemns? Christ Jesus is He who died, yes, rather who was raised, who is at the right hand of God, who also intercedes for us. [35] Who will separate us from the love of Christ? Will tribulation, or distress, or persecution, or famine, or nakedness, or peril, or sword? [36] Just as it is written, "For Your sake we are being put to death all day long; We were considered as sheep to be slaughtered." [37] But in all these things we overwhelmingly conquer through Him who loved us. [38] For I am convinced that neither death, nor life, nor angels, nor principalities, nor things present, nor things to come, nor powers, [39] nor height, nor depth, nor any other created thing, will be able to separate us from the love of God, which is in Christ Jesus our Lord. Romans 8:28-39 (NASB)

Consider the words of this passage:

God causes all things to work together for good to those who love him. Do you love God? Then you qualify! He knows how to take your worst and turn it into a tool in your hand. Your job is to allow Him to continue to conform you into the image of Jesus.

If God is for us, who is against us? It says that God gave up His own son so that He could justify us to our accusers, so He can freely give us all things. It says Jesus Himself intercedes for us. God is not only on your side, but He is ready to help you in all you do!

Nothing can separate us from the love of God. Nothing, not death or demons, or even ourselves can separate us from God's love. He adores you, and He is for you. Let that sink in!

Imagine for a moment that you are in a special school where only the best and the brightest are invited to attend. You are given a uniform that signals to the whole school that you belong among them. When you go to your classes you find that you are being trained to be an ambassador of peace and reconciliation to the nations. You are given a guide book, weapons of warfare, and a set of specialized gifts that will aide you in your journey. Is that appealing? That is who you are. You are part of the elect! God has called you and equipped you, and He is conforming you into the image of His Son, Jesus Christ. More than that, He loves you. He loves you so much that nothing can separate you from His love!

Take some time to ponder the words of Romans 8 and their impact on your life. Ask the Lord to show you any areas where your view of your life may need adjusting, and make it your goal to walk in the truth that is revealed.

Prayer:

Father, thank you for loving me more than words can say. Thank you for making me one of your very own, and for molding me to be more and more like Jesus. I ask you to reveal to me any ways that I see myself as less than you say that I am, and help me to embrace what you say about me. Thank you for loving me! In Jesus' Name, amen.

What does Romans 8 say about you?

_____

_____

_____

_____

_____

_____

_____

_____

_____

_____

_____

_____

_____

_____

_____

_____

15. Generational Sins

Have you ever heard someone say, "Oh, all the men on my mom's side of the family are like that.", or, "All the women in our family are strong-willed."? Do you see repetitive patterns, such as a tendency towards certain areas of sin or weaknesses? Is it a coincidence that your grandmother had fear issues, your mom has fear issues, and now you are also having fear issues? It may not be a coincidence at all. It may be a connected to a spiritual problem.

First, I must be very clear that Jesus took our curse when he died on the cross. Galatians 3: 13 says,

[13] Christ redeemed us from the curse of the Law, having become a curse for us—for it is written, "Cursed is everyone who hangs on a tree". (NASB)

The Old Testament gives details about curses under the Law, but we are not under the Law anymore, so the Old Testament way of thinking is no longer valid. Jesus died for all our sins. Period. But the enemy does seem to have ways to try to perpetuate the sins of our ancestors.

We may fall into his trap by perpetuating the wrong ways of thinking that are passed down to us by our family. For example, if our great-grandfather believed lies that were connected to sins in his life, he might have taught that erroneous thinking to our grandfather, who passed it on to our dad, who passed it down to us. Then we make decisions based on those lies that lead us into a similar temptation as our ancestor's. These sins can be anything from cheating on your taxes to dominating your spouse.

Sometimes we see a connection in the way events happen in our lives. For example, Great Uncle Bob lost his business due to a freak accident that left him in the hospital unable to work. Next, his son Jim Bob lost his farm in a tornado, then your cousin Robert lost his job to downsizing. It is not always clear why these things happen, but when a pattern emerges it may be connected to decisions made a long time ago. At that point, it would be a good idea to ask the Holy Spirit to show you if there is anything in your life or in your family line that can be forgiven. You may also ask your relatives if they know of anything that happened in the past that was unusual or kept hidden. You may find you need to ask forgiveness for your ancestors, and you may need to forgive someone who hurt them, as well.

Nehemiah is great example of someone who repented on behalf of his family and his nation. He confessed the sins of his ancestors, and he repented, or declared his intention to follow the Lord wholeheartedly. Then the Lord blessed him and gave him great favor, and eventually his nation was restored. (See Nehemiah 1:5-11)

Here are a few steps that I take to deal with generational issues:

1. Confess the sins of your ancestors and your own sins connected with it, known or unknown, and ask the Father for forgiveness.

2. Forgive your ancestors for the way their behavior has influenced your life.

3. Break all agreement with the sins or curses, and sever them from your life and the lives of your decedents. Jesus took every curse for us when He was crucified and now all authority belongs to Him, so in Jesus's Name command them to leave your lives.

4. Ask the Holy Spirit to come into every part of your life and fill you with His love and peace. Ask Him to teach you how to walk in new freedom, and how to see the world through His perspective.

5. Give thanks!

Prayer:

Father, I confess that my family members participated in (name the sins). I choose to forgive them for their sin and the way it has affected my life. I ask that you would forgive them, and also forgive me for any way that I have been associated with those sins. I break all agreement with these sins. I cut them off my life and the lives of my descendants for now and always, in Jesus' Name. Holy Spirit please come into every part of my life and fill me with your love and peace. Please teach me how to walk in freedom and see through your eyes. In Jesus' Name, amen!

16. Personal Sin

In a pool of water, in a quiet garden, sat a little green and yellow frog. She had a lily resting on the side of her head and a lopsided smile on her face. She had been sitting there eating flies in the shallow water for some time now. She knew that it was her own fault that she was there. She had made decisions, behaved in a way that she had been warned against. She had questioned the laws of the Maker, and she had reaped the consequences. Now she spent her days in the wet slimy pool, cursing herself for her foolish choices, and watching as regular people came to enjoy the beauty of the garden. All at once there was a stir in the air at the arrival of someone new. Everyone seemed to be drawn to him, and when the little frog caught a glimpse of him she knew why. He carried himself with quiet authority, and on his head, was a simple crown of gold. There was laughter in his eyes as he spoke to the people, and the little frog wished, for just a moment, that he would come over and talk to her. She quickly pushed such thoughts away, sure that someone like him would never even notice a little frog like herself. But just then everything went still. The prince brushed everyone aside as he turned his attention on her. Moving closer, he sought to catch her gaze. And then it happened. His eyes looked directly into hers. A warmth spread through her entire being, as he seemed to gaze into her very soul. He saw everything. In shame, the little frog broke the eye contact and looked away. But the prince did not turn away. Instead, he came closer, ever so gently. Quivering in anticipation, the little frog felt the flower slip from her head as the prince scooped her up into his royal hands. Then her eyes widened in amazement as he leaned down and lightly kissed her cheek, warts and all! Suddenly, everything changed. Suddenly, she was no longer a frog! In the blink of an eye she was transformed into a person again!

Having sin in our life can be very isolating. We know by the conviction of the Holy Spirit that we need to change what we are participating in, and it can feel like we are sitting in a wet slimy pool of sin. Maybe we promised Him over and over that we would never do whatever it is again, only to have failed once more. We expect Him to be exasperated with us, so we stay away. But Hebrews 4:15-16 states:

[15] For we do not have a high priest who cannot sympathize with our weaknesses, but One who has been tempted in all things as we are, yet without sin. [16] Therefore let us draw near with confidence to the throne of grace, so that we may receive mercy and find grace to help in time of need. (NASB)

The truth is that Jesus understands your struggle and wants to guide you into freedom. When you really look deeply into His heart you will be captivated all over again. He is love, and He is for you! He can see the potential of who you can become, and His purposes for you are still as strong as ever. He may give you a time out to deal with your issues, but He does not disqualify you.

If you have a hidden sin in your life, it is time for you to overcome it. You may need the help of a trusted advisor, someone who can pray with you and hold you accountable. You may need to take it in steps, and it may take some work to be fully free. But Jesus died and rose victorious, so nothing you face is too difficult for you to overcome when He is by your side. If you truly want to be free, He will make a way for you.

Prayer:

Jesus, thank you that you keep on loving me even when I have disappointed you over and over again. Thank you that you lived a life on earth so you can identify with my weaknesses. You know the places in my life where I have struggled with sin. You see the things that I have tried to hide from you and everyone else. I bring those things out in the open between you and I, and I lay them down at your feet. Thank you for your victory over all sin at the cross, and I ask that you will show me how to overcome these sins in your Name. Thank you for forgiving me and for loving me so much! In Your Name, amen!

17. Vows

Arthur was a man on a mission. He had an assignment from the Lord, and he intended to fulfill it! But every time Arthur started to move out towards his goal, something would happen to throw a wrench in his plans. Arthur decided to go on a fast and ask the Lord to show him anything in his life that was off. After a couple of days, Arthur remembered a promise that he had made to his mother. She had asked him to take her to see her sister, who lived too far away for his mother to drive by herself. Arthur had assured her that he would find time to take her, but he had been so busy trying to serve the Lord, that he had not done it. It was going to cost him at least a week of his time, and he dreaded the long drive to his aunt's home. But as he continued to pray, it became very clear to Arthur that the Lord was requiring him to be a man of his word, and to honor his mother and aunt. So, Arthur did as he had promised. Soon after that, Arthur found himself fulfilling his mission.

If you are stuck like Arthur, ask the Lord if there are any promises that you have made to others, or maybe even to Him. You may find that you, too, have something to finish before you can move on.

Sydney made a different kind of promise when she was eighteen. She thought she had the world all figured out, and she despised her parents for their old-fashioned beliefs. As she left home she made a vow that she didn't need them and that she would find someone to make a new family with. After several years passed, Sydney began to understand her parents' point of view. She made attempts to get close to her parents again, and there was some progress. But she always felt like something got in the way. To complicate matters, Sydney's teenage son had a very similar attitude towards her as she once had towards her parents. One Sunday, during the closing prayer, the pastor invited people to break agreement with negative vows that had been made. Sydney decided to pray the prayer, and to ask forgiveness for dishonoring her parents. The next time Sydney saw her mother, she felt a love and understanding for her that she had not felt in a long time. Over the next months, she found her relationship with her parents growing into a stronger and more trusting adult relationship, and it filled an emptiness that she had not been able to identify. She also found it easier to communicate with her son, which opened the door to a stronger relationship with him.

Vows, or strong intents of the heart, that are made in anger or judgment can become a trap for us. Phrases like, "I will never...", or "I swear I will not be like..." can be very hard to live up to, and we find ourselves becoming the exact thing we swore we would never be. By their nature, they indicate that there is probably someone who you need to forgive or to come out of judgment towards. When you see the very judgment that you made about someone else being made about you, it is a good time repent of any judgments you are holding on to.

There can be vows that seem positive. You can swear that you will accomplish your dreams, or find a cure for a disease, or lose weight by next summer... But the

Lord advised that we refrain from any kind of oaths. Matt. 5:33-37 says:

33 "Again, you have heard that it was said to the people long ago, 'Do not break your oath, but fulfill to the Lord the vows you have made.' 34 But I tell you, do not swear an oath at all: either by heaven, for it is God's throne; 35 or by the earth, for it is his footstool; or by Jerusalem, for it is the city of the Great King. 36 And do not swear by your head, for you cannot make even one hair white or black. 37 All you need to say is simply 'Yes' or 'No'; anything beyond this comes from the evil one. (NASB)

Take some time today to ask the Lord if there are any vows or intentions of your heart that He would like for you to reconsider.

Prayer:

Father, thank you that you never forget your promises to me. I ask that you show me any place in my life where I have made promises that you would like for me to either fulfill, or ask forgiveness for. I also ask that you would forgive me for any vows or intents of my heart that have been made in judgment. I chose to forgive the person or persons who inspired those judgments and I ask you to forgive me for holding anything against them. I renounce all vows and chose to make my answers simply, 'Yes' and 'No', just like Jesus advised. Thank you for loving me! In Jesus' Name, amen.

18. Idols

Picture a newly married couple moving into their first home. They are very much in love. He brings in stuff that belongs to him and she brings in things that are hers. They begin to discuss where they are going to put everything, and they are having a wonderful day - until she insists on leaving the guest room alone. When he asks about her plans for that room, she says that her old boyfriend is moving in with them. Sure enough, the guy pulls up in his old pick-up truck with his dusty old suitcase and a huge smile. As you can imagine, the bridegroom is not too happy with this scenario! But this is what it is like when you hold on to idols. They interfere with your relationship with the Lord. You and Jesus may spend personal time in the early or late hours, but the rest of the time your old best friend is there, too. He is always influencing, and stealing moments meant for your Bridegroom. He could be any form of idolatry...fear, anger, gossip, technology, television, hobbies, drugs, anything that you find your identity in, anything you turn to when you are challenged or upset. Colossians 3:5-10 states:

[5]Put to death, therefore, whatever belongs to your earthly nature: sexual immorality, impurity, lust, evil desires and greed, which is idolatry. [6]Because of these, the wrath of God is coming. [7]You used to walk in these ways, in the life you once lived. [8]But now you must also rid yourselves of all such things as these: anger, rage, malice, slander, and filthy language from your lips. [9]Do not lie to each other, since you have taken off your old self with its

practices [10] and have put on the new self, which is being renewed in knowledge in the image of its Creator. (NASB)

Sometimes idols are in the form of another person or accomplishment, that in which you put all your hopes for the future. Hopes for whatever it is that you think will make everything in your life finally complete. Some people put so much hope into their future spouse that they think when they finally meet the perfect person, their lives will come together. The result is that they can never be satisfied with a regular person. Others put all their hope in their kids, investing all their time and energy planning for their kid's future. They forget about living their own lives with the Bridegroom today. But putting all your hope in a person, a job or ministry, or simply being acknowledged by certain people, will cause a rift between you and only one who can truly satisfy your heart and give you purpose. This was what Adam and Eve did. They questioned whether God was enough to meet their needs, entertaining the thought that He might be withholding from them. Then they put their trust in another voice. (See Genesis 3)

Hebrews 12: 1-2 says:

Therefore, we also, since we are surrounded by so great a cloud of witnesses, let us lay aside every weight, and the sin which so easily ensnares *us*, and let us run with endurance the race that is set before us, [2] looking unto Jesus, the author and finisher of *our* faith, who for the joy that was set before Him endured the cross, despising the shame, and has sat down at the right hand of the throne of God. (NKJV)

The posture of sitting indicates to us that Jesus is at rest. In other words, He has accomplished all that He set out to do when He took back what Adam and Eve lost in the garden. If He has all authority, He can meet your needs. The question is, are you willing to put your complete trust in Him? If so, it is time to lay down your hold on other people or things that you have been putting your trust in, and ask Him to put those things in their proper perspective. Also, take time to ask Him if there is anything that you need to let go of completely, any ex-partners that you have been keeping in the background just in case you need them. Make the Lord your one true Bridegroom!

Prayer:

Jesus, thank you that you have so much patience with me. I ask that you show me any places in my life where I have allowed other things be the source I rely on for comfort or identity. I ask that you would forgive me for not going to you for those things. I also ask that you would show me any places where I have put people or accomplishments above you in my life. I ask that you will put them in proper perspective for me, so that I can truly make you the central focus of my life. I want to love you above all else! Thank you for loving me! In Your Name, amen.

19. Fear of Man

When Lottie turned forty she bought a condominium. She had been saving for ten years, and since she had not married she decided it was time to buy her dream home on her own. She decorated it perfectly. Anyone who came in would think that it was a model home. In fact, she would joke that it looked like an advertisement for the local furniture store. Then one day an old friend came to visit her from out of town. Her friend complemented her on the beautiful home she had established. But then she commented that she didn't see anything of Lottie's personal life reflected in the paintings or decorations, and asked Lottie why that was. As Lottie took time to reflect on the answer to her friend's question, she began to realize that she had been concerned about what other people would say or think if her home wasn't perfect. When she prayed about the matter, she felt the Lord agreed with her conclusion. So, Lottie went shopping. She found a picture of Jesus on sale and put it in a prominent place in her living room. She found a few other pictures that reflected her love of bright colors, and she put up pictures of friends and family. To her surprise, Lottie began to feel much more 'at home' in her own home. Then she began to look at other areas of her life as well.

King Saul was a man who struggled all his life with being concerned about what other people thought. When Samuel prophesied to him in 1 Samuel 9 that he would be the new king, he responded by saying that he was the least of his family, which was the least of his tribe, which was the smallest of all the tribes. Since Saul was a tall man for his day, we know he was concerned about something other than his stature. He had self-esteem issues, and he made his choices in life based on those insecurities, or fears. He was jealous when David excelled above him on the battlefield, and tried to kill David more than once. I believe that his jealousy was rooted in the fear that people would find him inadequate. In 1 Samuel 15, Saul disobeyed God to please the people, and that was when God decided to get another king.

Many people have areas in their lives where they are more interested in fitting in than they are in standing out. Romans 12:2 tells us:

2 And do not be conformed to this world, but be transformed by the renewing of your mind, so that you may prove what the will of God is, that which is good and acceptable and perfect.

In my experience, the fear of man is often associated with the fear of rejection. We want to impress other people so we will be accepted and loved. It all pertains to how we see ourselves, much like Saul.

Sometimes dealing with fear can be as simple as realizing that we are in agreement with it, and changing direction. Like Lottie, we can simply make changes. However, there are other situations that require a little more work. If you are dealing with crippling fear, anything that results in extreme behavior, I suggest that you seek out people that can help you. (See pages 8-9 for more details.)

Take time today to ask the Holy Spirit if there are any areas of your life where you have fallen into the trap of pleasing people, rather than being the person that God has called you to be. Then take time to be 'transformed by the renewing of your mind' as Romans 12 says. Read Romans 8:28-39, and remind yourself who you are and how much God loves you!

Prayer:

Father, thank you for your great love for me! I ask that you show me any place in my life where I have been more concerned about what people think about me than what you think of me. I also ask you to forgive me for putting what they think first in my life. I chose to break all agreement with the fear of man and the fear of rejection, and I embrace your love for me. Thank you that your perfect love casts out all fear! In Jesus' Name, amen!

20. Control

One time I was driving on a highway in Oklahoma right after a storm. There was ice on the road, and despite my best efforts, the car spun out of control. It only lasted about four seconds, but they seemed to last an eternity. It was terrifying until I came to a stop, with my heart pounding a mile a minute, and I gave thanks for coming through it alive in one piece. Being out of control can be a horrible feeling!

When a child experiences that kind of feeling, due to divorce issues, abuse, or even a less severe incident, they sometimes cling to the things that they *can* control. Years later, as adults, they find themselves shutting down or having panic attacks when their world doesn't work the way they want it to. You hear comments like, "He is so controlling", or "She always has to have her own way". This may be the result of a wound deep down that needs to be healed, including the fear and trauma that came with it. The key here is to recognize the source of the fear that is threatening to bring everything down around the person. If you experience fear based on a severely traumatic event or series of events, it would be best if you dealt with this subject in a setting where you have the support of other people. (See pages 8-9 for more details.)

If you struggle with minor issues concerning a need for control, ask the Lord when this began and who you need to forgive. Once you forgive them, you may need to forgive yourself and maybe even God. Next, ask Him to forgive you for being controlling and lay it down at his feet. Break off all agreement with control and fear, and command that they leave your life. Then, ask the Holy Spirit to show you the truth. Finally, ask the Holy Spirit to fill you with peace.

One area where some people don't recognize they are grasping for control revolves around asking for prayer. See if this scenario sounds familiar:

James is searching to find his purpose in life so he prays, reads his Bible, and goes to church every Sunday. He knows who the strongest prayer people are in his church, so he often stands in line to get one of them to pray over him. He hopes that they will hear from God and tell him the answers to his questions. When a speaker comes to visit, he gets in that person's prayer line as well. He often feels like he is overlooked or rushed, and sometimes gets upset over what they pray. In fact, James is never quite satisfied with the answers he gets, so he keeps on in this process feeling misunderstood by people and forgotten by God.

The issue for people like James, is that he is going to people to fill a need that God is supposed to fill. He is not trusting that the Lord will answer him, so he is trying to make it happen himself. When we are desperately trying to find the person with the answer for us, when we are repeatedly looking to people, we are operating out of control instead of trust. We are, in essence, saying, "God, you are not meeting my needs so I am going to look to your people to force you to answer me." We are also operating out of a need to prove ourselves, both to God and man. Control is often connected to the fear of man.

So, what is the answer to this dilemma? First, you need to go back to the foundation of your faith and start building your relationship with the Father based on what *He* has done for *you*, not the other way around. Read Galatians 4 and remember that you are a child of promise, not a slave to fear. Ask Him to encounter you, to show you who you are in Him, and to teach you to trust Him. If you have any promises or prophetic words from Him, hold on to them and trust that He will do what He promised. Then, make sure you are in a home church where you can be a part of a group of people who support each other within healthy boundaries. Finally, take a step of faith and *wait on Him.*

Take a moment to pray and ask the Holy Spirit if there are any areas of control in your life that He wants to address. If there are, ask Him to show you where there is a lack of trust, and then to show you the truth.

Prayer:

Father, thank you for loving me even when I don't trust you. I ask that you show me any places in my life where I have tried to control my life instead of looking to you. I break all agreement with fear, trauma, and control, and I ask you to forgive me for allowing them into my life. I ask that you would fill me anew with your love, and teach me how to trust you. I want to know you and your love for me in a deep and personal way. Thank you that your perfect love casts out all fear. In Jesus' Name, amen!

21. A Royal Priesthood, A Holy Nation

[9] But you are a chosen race, a royal priesthood, a holy nation, a people for God's own possession, so that you may proclaim the excellencies of Him who has called you out of darkness into His marvelous light; [10] for you once were not a people, but now you are the people of God; you had not received mercy, but now you have received mercy. [11] Beloved, I urge you as aliens and strangers to abstain from fleshly lusts which wage war against the soul. [12] Keep your behavior excellent among the Gentiles, so that in the thing in which they slander you as evildoers, they may because of your good deeds, as they observe them, glorify God in the day of visitation. 1 Peter 2:9-12 (NASB)

My sister and her family spent several years living in London, England. While they enjoyed their experiences there, they were still aliens living in a foreign land. They had to learn new vocabulary, figure out how to work machines that looked slightly different from the ones they were used to, and remember to drive on the opposite side of the road. Every year towards the end of November, my sister would get just a little homesick for the United States. Since the British don't celebrate Thanksgiving, there were no pictures of turkey dinners or pilgrims to be seen! But there were other Americans in her church, and they would gather to support each other in times like those. Years later, those same people are still very close friends. They have become a 'people', or a family, through their experiences together.

In a similar way, we are like travelers from another country living in this world. Our home is where God dwells, and we are simply visiting so that we can bring His light to this place. We don't do things the same way as the people who live here do. We resist the lust of this world because it is in such conflict with who we have become. We follow the ways of our Father, and He gives us the answers that will help make this world more like His. Our mandate is to reveal His love and to bring reconciliation and healing to the nations. Like my sister and her friends, we need each other. It can be lonely and difficult to live in two worlds at odds with each other. We need the support of God's family to remind ourselves of who we are and why we are here. 2 Corinthians 5:17-19 states:

[17] Therefore if anyone is in Christ, he is a new creature; the old things passed away; behold, new things have come. [18] Now all these things are from God, who reconciled us to Himself through Christ and gave us the ministry of reconciliation, [19] namely, that God was in Christ reconciling the world to Himself, not counting their trespasses against them, and He has committed to us the word of reconciliation. [20] Therefore, we are ambassadors for Christ, as though God were making an appeal through us; we beg you on behalf of Christ, be reconciled to God. [21] He made Him who knew no sin to be sin on our behalf, so that we might become the righteousness of God in Him. (NASB)

Take some time to ponder what these two Scriptures say about who you are, and write down your thoughts:

_____

_____

_____

_____

_____

_____

_____

_____

_____

_____

_____

_____

_____

_____

_____

_____

_____

_____

Prayer:

Father, thank you for making me a new creation. You have shown me mercy and brought me out of darkness into your light. You call me royal, as in part of your own family, and I have a place among your people. I am part of a priesthood that ministers to you, and you have called me to bring reconciliation between you and the people of this world. Please help me to be an ambassador for you, to be strong in resisting the lust of this world, and to work with your people. In Jesus' Name, amen.

22. Anger

Jaden is a funny little boy who is just about to turn five years old. When he gets frustrated, he doesn't quite know what to do. So, he says, "When I go home I'm going to kick the couch!" Now Jaden is really cute, and I am glad that he has the self-control to wait until he gets home to kick something. But anger is not cute, nor does it usually come with self-control. Ephesians 4:26-27 states:

[26]Be angry, and yet do not sin; do not let the sun go down on your anger, [27] and do not give the devil an opportunity. (NASB)

This passage makes it clear that sometimes we will be angry. The key is that we don't sin in our anger.

People struggle with anger for different reasons. If someone grew up in an angry household, there are probably people they need to forgive. There may also be some generational sins connected to it. If you are dealing with abusive behavior, road rage, or PTSD, it is time to get the support of the Body of Christ and ask for help. (See pages 8-9 for more details.) If you are dealing with a lot of frustration, it would help for you to sit down and walk through the process of your day, asking the Holy Spirit to point out where the triggers are. Then ask Him for a game plan for overcoming the frustration. There may be some people you need to forgive, including yourself, or you might need to adjust your expectations of yourself or others. Whatever it is, invite Him into the middle of it and be open to making changes. God does not bring things into our lives to frustrate us, but He will use the opportunity to show us things about ourselves that He would like to see improved.

A subtle area of anger in many of our lives is connected to entitlement, where people think they are owed something and consequently justify their anger. Here is an example:

Sarah must return something to the local department store. While she is standing in line, one of the people who is at the cash register is painfully slow. It seems like this worker doesn't know what she is doing, and she keeps interrupting the other worker to help her with different things. As Sarah is waiting she begins to roll her eyes whenever this happens. She shakes her head in disgust and sighs deeply. When she finally gets to the register she is impatient and has a very negative attitude with the worker. Then Sarah stomps off, leaving the worker feeling inadequate and humiliated.

Does this sound familiar? Why is it that some of us feel like it is our right to complain about other people's flaws? We feel justified for our poor behavior when we are inconvenienced. Ephesians 4 continues in verses 31-32:

31 Let all bitterness and wrath and anger and clamor and slander be put away from you, along with all malice. 32 Be kind to one another, tender-hearted, forgiving each other, just as God in Christ also has forgiven you. (NASB)

Take a moment to ask the Lord if there is any place for anger or entitlement in your life. If you need to, ask forgiveness from the Lord and anyone else that comes to mind. Then change your mind set by forgiving whomever you need to forgive, and breaking agreement with anger, control, entitlement, and/or whatever else the Lord brings to your mind.

Prayer:

Father, thank you for loving me even when I get angry. I ask that you show me any place in my life where I need to forgive someone. I also ask you to show me if I have come into agreement with entitlement. I break all agreement with anger, control, bitterness, and entitlement, and I ask you to forgive me for allowing them into my life. I ask that you would fill me deeply with your love, and teach me how to see people through your eyes. In Jesus' Name, amen!

23. Shame

My friend had a small dog names Sushi. She was a cute little thing, but her fur was a little heavy for our climate. Every once in a while, her owner would take her to get groomed, where they would shave off most of Sushi's hair. When I would come to visit, Sushi would jump and bark and act very happy to see me. But when she had just been groomed, she would lower her head and her tail and slink away. She was reacting in shame.

People are like that, too. When we feel naked or exposed we shrink back and hide. In fact, shame can be one of the worst enemies we face simply due to the way it isolates us. It is hard to ask for help when we don't feel safe telling someone what we need help with. But Jesus is neither shocked or deterred by your shame. He took it upon Himself when he went to the cross, open for the world to see, so that you can be free. Remember Hebrews 12:2:

...fixing our eyes on Jesus, the author and perfector of faith, who for the joy set before Him endured the cross, despising the shame, and has sat down at the right hand of the throne of God. (NASB)

He had the strength to endure the cross because He knew that you and I could be set free from that despicable shame. Now He sits in the place of authority, and it is His great joy to see you find that freedom! In Isaiah 61, the passage Jesus said that He had come to fulfill in Luke 4:18, the Lord says:

Instead of your shame you will have a double portion, And instead of humiliation they will shout for joy over their portion. Therefore, they will possess a double portion in their land. Everlasting joy will be theirs. Isaiah 61:7 (NASB)

You see? He is waiting to exchange our shame for a double portion, for a place in the land (instead of hiding), and for great joy!

Toby was a man who was working hard to get free from the guilt and shame of his own past. He dealt with a lot of anger and fear, forgiving the people who had hurt him as well as himself. He had achieved a lot of freedom, but he still hung his head and kept to himself. One day in a men's group, Toby admitted that his dad had gone to jail for theft when he was a little boy. As it turned out, both sides of the family had reacted very badly and a blanket of shame had settled over him and his parents ever since. That day Toby was able to forgive both his dad and his family, and he broke agreement with the accuser who told him that he had to walk ashamed and inferior for the rest of his life. Toby felt a huge weight lift from him, and he walked with a new confidence.

Shame can come into our lives through a variety of circumstances. Many people have childhood experiences that have impacted them in ways they don't even think about any more. Perhaps there was a comment made by a teacher, a neighbor, or a relative that causes you to shy away from certain circumstances. Or, maybe it was something more severe. Whatever the cause, you can get free from shame by recognizing that Jesus bore your shame on the cross. Break all agreement with the lie that says you have to live ashamed. There is no condemnation for you in Christ Jesus!

Prayer:

Jesus, thank you that you took my shame upon yourself when you went to the cross. You see the places in my life where I have been ashamed and you have forgiven me for my role in any sin. I ask that you would help me to let go of shame, and to open myself again to joy and purpose. Open my eyes to see myself as you see me. Thank you for loving me! In Your Name, amen!

24. Reclaiming Your Voice

Renee grew up in a small town where she only had a couple of churches to choose from. When she was in middle school, she began to have dreams that would often come true. She talked to her pastor about it, and was told that she must be doing something to attract the attention of the devil. The pastor treated her like there was something wrong with her after that, so Renee quickly decided to keep her dreams to herself. Finally, when she was in college, Renee met a young man named Kevin who also had dreams. He shared about his experiences with the Holy Spirit and explained that having dreams from God is a gift. Renee began to embrace her prophetic gift, and during her winter vacation she decided to share one of her dreams with the people of her home church. Sadly, the pastor and many of the older members of her church told her that she was behaving inappropriately and that women were not allowed to speak during a service without getting it approved ahead of time. Renee was so humiliated that she chose never to speak about her dreams again. Ten years later, when Renee finally found a church where the prophetic gifts and women in ministry were both embraced, she found it was hard to remember her dreams and wondered if she had lost her gift for good.

It is not uncommon to find people who have shut down an area of gifting or creativity due to a negative person of influence in their life. Sometimes it was a teacher who put them on the spot, mocking them for not knowing an answer, or correcting them in front of their peers. It may have been the result of having a parent or guardian who called them stupid or worthless. Or, it may be the words of a pastor or spiritual leader, like in the scenario above. For me, it was isolation and my perceived lack of support. Whatever the case, the resulting emotional turmoil was enough to 'steal their voice'. But there is hope! It's not too late to get your voice back.

For clarity, when I say 'voice' I am referring to your ability to communicate with confidence and freedom. This can be as simple as being able to give your opinion, and it can be as complicated as interpreting a prophetic vision. It can be music, dance, poetry, painting, photography, and so many other expressions. It is being able to convey the truth of God's goodness in whatever means that He has put within you. The enemy may have tried to steal it from you, but God has a purpose for you and your voice! 2 Timothy 1:6-7 says:

6 Therefore I remind you to stir up the gift of God which is in you through the laying on of my hands. 7 For God has not given us a spirit of fear, but of power and of love and of a sound mind. (NASB)

Fear does not have to own your voice, but there are a few steps to taking it back. If you have shut down due to the words or action of others, you will need to start by forgiving them. Then you need to break all agreement with fear and take back your voice. Memorize verse seven above and declare it over yourself as often as you need to be reminded of the truth, and spend a lot of time worshipping the Lord for his goodness. Finally, practice. Take the first steps to making your voice heard with people that you trust. Then look for places where there are people who need encouragement and practice on them. Make your focus encouragement, exhortation, and comfort to the Body of Christ, and you will see people blessed!

Prayer:

Father, thank you for the gifts you have given me, even the ones that I have buried. I ask that you show me any place in my life where I have shut down because of fear. I also ask you to show me if there is anyone I need to forgive. I choose to forgive all who hurt me and rejected my efforts. I break all agreement with fear, and I ask you to forgive me for allowing fear to rule my life. I ask that you would fill me with confidence in who you made me to be, and teach me how to move forward in the gifts you have put within me. Thank you for being so good! In Jesus' Name, amen!

25. Playing it Safe

[28] Peter said to Him, "Lord, if it is You, command me to come to You on the water." [29] And He said, "Come!" And Peter got out of the boat, and walked on the water and came toward Jesus. Matthew 14:28-29 (NASB)

Several years ago, I write a children's book. It was good, and I tried to get it illustrated a few times. But for some reason it never worked out. After a while I decided that it must not be time to get it published and put it on the shelf. I had tried other creative ventures, as well as ministry opportunities, but nothing had been very successful. The Lord had used those experiences to teach me that my identity is not in what I do, but in Him. I was successful at being an intercessor, so at some point I settled there. But I had an empty place within me. Then one day I was in a worship service at my church when I got a very clear prophetic picture in my head. I was standing under a pier looking longingly out over the ocean. I wanted to go out and have adventures so badly! Then I heard that still small voice within my heart whisper to me, "What are you hiding from? Are you willing to trust Me?" I knew it was an important moment, and I chose in that moment to say yes. "Yes!" Then in the picture I saw a speed boat coming really fast towards me. Somehow I knew it was the Holy Spirit. He barely slowed down to let me on. Then we went speeding out onto the open waters. It was exhilarating, and He was just as excited as I was! That day I decided to look for another illustrator.

I wish I could say that it all worked out and that my book was a best seller. It didn't work quite like that, and the book is still in process. But, saying 'yes' to trying opened other things in my heart as well. I decided to go to ministry school, and from there doors began to open a little at a time. It was the stepping out that made the difference for me. I took a long look at my life and decided that I was tired of playing it safe, of making excuses as to why I couldn't do what was the deep desire of my heart.

Are you tired of playing it safe? Do you have some hidden, or not so hidden, dreams that you have never dared try to fulfill? Maybe you have tried and fallen flat on your face. Were you trying to prove your worth the first time around? Have you learned to find your identity in Him? Are you willing to trust the Lord to take you where He wants you to go? It may not look like what you have dreamed of, but it will be good.

Today I would like you to take some time to examine your heart and explore these questions. Take a few moments to sit quietly and listen to His still small voice asking you, "What are you hiding from?" and "Are you willing to trust Me?" Ask Him where you need to start, and dare to formulate a plan with Him.

If you are someone who has already stepped out and are living your dreams, you may need to ask if there is any change of direction that He is asking you to make. Or, ask if there are any people in your life that need to be encouraged to step out. There are probably some folks at your church, or in your fellowship group, that would benefit from your experience. Take some time to pray for them, and then set up a time to meet with them to bring encouragement.

Prayer:

Father, thank you for the desires that you have put deep within my heart. I ask that you show me any places in my life where I have been too discouraged or afraid to pursue my dreams. I also ask you to show me if there is anyone I need to forgive, including myself. I choose to forgive all who hurt me and rejected my efforts. I break all agreement with fear and discouragement, and I ask you to forgive me for allowing them to rule my life. I ask that you would fill me with confidence in who you made me to be, and teach me how to move forward towards the dreams you have put within me. Today I am choosing to trust you! In Jesus' Name, amen!

Plans for stepping out:

_____

_____

_____

_____

_____

_____

_____

_____

_____

26. Memorials

Imagine the large living room window of a cabin in the mountains, overlooking a beautiful vista. The view is open and limitless. The sky is blue and the trees are tall and green in the distance. Now notice that there are all sorts of headstones in the front yard. Some of them are so tall that they block your view. Those headstones are the memorials that you have set up, reminders of past successes, struggles, and failures. They are the things that define you, and you are wear them with resolve. But they are a graveyard...and they are blocking your sightlines. Are you willing to move them out of the way? Will you allow the Lord to show you who He says you are today? It is time to clear those things away!

Everyone has failures in their past. Some people know how to make them a life lesson and move on, but some use their failures to define who they cannot be. The 'I can't' attitude may limit what the Lord can do in a life. Now that you have let go of so many negative influences, those impossible things may just be possible. Today is a good day to re-evaluate those areas where you have given up. Ask the Lord if you are believing less of yourself because of past mistakes, and dare to allow yourself to learn and grow. Stir up your courage and ask if He wants you to try something new. Philippians 4:13 says:

[13] I can do all things through Christ who strengthens me. (NKJV)

Ask Him to show you small steps that you can take, and try again!

Surprisingly, you may have some memorials that you didn't know were there. In Exodus 17, the people of Israel needed water and God told Moses to strike a rock. The water flowed in miraculous wonder, strengthening the people's trust in Moses as a representative of God. Then, in Numbers 20, we see the people in need of water again. But this time God tells Moses to speak to the rock. Unfortunately, Moses hits the rock again and God is displeased. Because of this Moses was not allowed into the Promised Land. Moses had put his confidence in what had worked in the past, the thing that had won him the people's confidence. I can imagine the thoughts going through his mind at that moment. "Did I hear Him wrong? These people will be really angry if I don't get them some water...I will do what worked last time." He held too closely to what had happened before. But it is my experience that the Lord rarely does things the same way twice. If we get too confident in our accomplishments, put trust in our knowledge rather than keeping our eyes and ears on the Lord, we may miss the subtle change in His direction.

There may be areas of your life where you have excelled that are not the focus in the coming season of your life. For example, a celebrated football player may be the fastest, most agile of his time. But when he transitions from being a player to being a coach, running fast may not be much help. His knowledge of the game and his experiences will contribute to what he does. However, he will need to rely on strategy, instruction, and encouragement based on the needs of his players to be an effective coach. For us to be effective, we need to be in tune with what the Holy Spirit is saying about the season we are in. He will gladly give us the strategies and direction we need, if we are open to change and new ideas.

Take some time today to ask the Holy Spirit to reveal any places in your life where you have set up memorial stones. Then ask Him to help you put them in the proper perspective.

1. Failures that I have let define me:

_____

_____

_____

_____

_____

2. Successes I put my trust in:

_____

_____

_____

_____

_____

Prayer:

Father, thank you for the journey of my life. You have walked with me through the good and the bad, and you always love me the same. I ask that you show me any places in my life where I have assumed that I know what to do and not consulted you. Please reveal any preconceived ideas of who I am that don't align with who you say I am. Please help me to see and embrace the truth. Thank you for helping me to put my past successes and failures into proper perspective, so I can walk forward, ready to accomplish all you have for me. Thank you! In Jesus' Name, amen.

27. The Desires of Your Heart

Just as we had to let go of past successes and failures, there are times in our lives where we need to loosen our grasp on our old dreams to make way for new ones. Psalm 37:4 says:

Delight yourself in the Lord and He will give you the desires of your heart. (NASB)

I believe that this can be read two different ways. If we delight in Him he will give us the things we desire, and if we delight in Him He will put desires in our hearts that align with His.

The more time I spend with the Lord, the more I want to be running after the things He is going after. Sometimes this means laying down my dreams and allowing Him to restructure them. As you have been going through this process of leaving old stuff behind, I assume that there have been some breakthroughs. This is a great time to lay your dreams before God's throne and ask Him to help you re-examine them. You can take out the old stuff that doesn't need to be there anymore, and add in whatever He wants.

I am not asking you to give up your dreams. If you are being stirred by memories of someone who quashed your hopes, it may be an indication that you have need to forgive someone. You know how to do that, so forgive them and get free! I am simply asking you to do a little house cleaning. It's kind of like putting on your favorite coat. You put your hand in the pocket and to your surprise...there is an old sandwich from last season. You dig a little deeper and find a gritty old tube of lip balm, two cough drops, and a wadded-up tissue. Ick! It is time to throw those things out. You may find a pair of gloves in there that will need to stay in your pocket. Not everything will need to go! He put those dreams in you to begin with. Put your trust in Him as the one who knows how to navigate the future and who has your best interest at heart.

Take some time today to sit and talk with the Lord about your dreams. First, write them out. Then, ask Him to show you any parts of them that were influenced by old ways of thinking, and have Him show you any adjustments that need to be made. Finally, dare to ask Him if He has any new dreams for you!

Dream 1:

_____

_____

_____

_____

_____

Dream 2:

_____

_____

_____

_____

_____

Dream 3:

_____

_____

_____

_____

_____

New Dream:

_____

_____

_____

_____

_____

Prayer:

Jesus, thank you for the dreams that you have placed in my heart. I ask you to show me how to pursue them in a way that keeps you in the center of them. I ask for the grace to embrace the process of preparation that accompanies seeing those dreams fulfilled. I put my trust in you! In Your Name, amen.

28. Good News

In Luke 4:18, Jesus read from the scroll of Isaiah, (Isaiah 61), and said that He was the fulfillment of that promise. He said He had come to set the prisoners free, and He has continued to do that for us during these last weeks. Let's look at what the whole chapter says:

The Spirit of the Lord God is upon me, because the Lord has anointed me to bring good news to the afflicted; He has sent me to bind up the brokenhearted, to proclaim liberty to captives and freedom to prisoners; [2] To proclaim the favorable year of the Lord and the day of vengeance of our God; To comfort all who mourn, [3] to grant those who mourn in Zion, giving them a garland instead of ashes, the oil of gladness instead of mourning, the mantle of praise instead of a spirit of fainting. Isaiah 61:1-3a (NASB)

It is my hope and expectation that the Lord has made some significant exchanges, giving beauty for ashes, and freedom from captivity in your life. Now it is time to put on the oil of gladness and the garment of praise! This is what He says about your future:

So they will be called oaks of righteousness, the planting of the Lord, that He may be glorified. [4] Then they will rebuild the ancient ruins, they will raise up the former devastations; and they will repair the ruined cities, the desolations of many generations. [5] Strangers will stand and pasture your flocks, and foreigners will be your farmers and your vinedressers. [6] But you will be called the priests of the Lord; you will be spoken of as ministers of our God. You will eat the wealth of nations, and in their riches you will boast. [7] Instead of your shame you will have a double portion, and instead of humiliation they will shout for joy over their portion.

Therefore, they will possess a double portion in their land, everlasting joy will be theirs. [8] For I, the Lord, love justice, I hate robbery in the burnt offering; and I will faithfully give them their recompense and make an everlasting covenant with them. [9] Then their offspring will be known among the nations, and their descendants in the midst of the peoples. All who see them will recognize them because they are the offspring whom the Lord has blessed. Isaiah 61:3b-9 (NASB)

Take a moment to digest what you just read. This is God's purpose for your life. When Jesus came to redeem us it was to restore an everlasting covenant with us, to make us His family. He made God, *His* father, *our* father. The Father loves to bless and lavish His love on His kids, and as you are seeking Him and loving Him He will naturally pour His love back onto you. That is worth celebrating!

[10] I will rejoice greatly in the Lord, my soul will exult in my God; for He has clothed me with garments of salvation, he has wrapped me with a robe of righteousness, as a bridegroom decks himself with a garland, and as a bride adorns herself with her jewels. [11] For as the earth brings forth its sprouts, and as a garden causes the things sown in it to spring up, so the Lord God will cause righteousness and praise to spring up before all the nations. Isaiah 61:10-11 (NASB)

If you are being blessed by this passage of Scripture, I suggest you go to Isaiah 62 and continue. Remember that there were no chapter breaks when Isaiah wrote this!

Take a few moments to write down the things that stood out to you as you read this passage. Trust that the

Holy Spirit is highlighting those things so that you will hold on to the words as His promises to you. Lift your head and walk tall, knowing that His plans and purposes for you are for your good!

Prayer:

Jesus, thank you for coming into this world to set the captives free! Thank you for the way you have taken my areas of brokenness and turned them into places of hope and peace. I ask that you would help me become someone who will bless you by the way I live my life. Thank you for blessing me so abundantly! In Your Name, amen!

What stands out to you in Isaiah 61?

_____

_____

_____

_____

_____

_____

_____

_____

_____

_____

_____

29. Maintaining Freedom

We began this journey with the picture of the Good Shepherd cleaning our feet. We spent time forgiving others and ourselves, breaking agreements with lies, and readjusting our thinking about our lives to reflect the way the Father sees us. Now it is time for us to prepare to move forward, holding firm to our peace, and maintaining our freedom. There are a few suggestions that will help you along the way:

Read the Bible as often as you can, daily if possible. – The best way to keep your mind focused on the truth is to fill it with God's Word. It is a good idea to come back to the gospels often. Jesus lived his life as an example of what the Father is like, so reading about Him helps to keep our perspective healthy. Also, keep in mind that we live in a covenant of grace, meaning the Law of religious control is not for us. We obey because of our great love for God and His love for us, not because we are afraid He will punish us. Remember that as you read the Old Testament, and ask the Lord to help you find Him within it each time you read.

Pray – 1 Thessalonians 5:17 says to pray without ceasing. This doesn't mean should kneel for twelve hours a day. I believe that this means that you can have a running dialog with the Lord as you go about your day. Include Him in your decisions, be quick to get back on track when you mess up, and set aside some time to talk to Him directly. Daniel prayed morning, noon, and night, and David prayed on his bed. Find what works for you.

Worship – When you truly worship, all your focus goes back on the Lord. When we *magnify* Him, we recognize how much bigger He is than our problems. When we worship with a group of people it can be even more powerful. When we are truly worshipping, He draws near and His presence is more easy to sense. Daily worship will refresh your spirit and strengthen you to move forward.

Fellowship – Even if you have been hurt in the past, you need to be around other believers. Proverbs 27:17 says:

As iron sharpens iron, so a man sharpens the countenance of his friend. (NKJV)

When we are endeavoring to maintain a balanced and truthful perspective about ourselves and our lives, we need trusted people around us who will tell us if what we are saying sounds a little off. Also, if we find someone who needs to hear about our freedom to get free themselves, it will strengthen and encourage us as we are sharing it. God made us to need each other.

Make smart choices - If you go back to the places where you once dwelt in darkness, don't be surprised if some of your old 'friends' are there to greet you. For example, if you have struggled with self-pity because you are divorced, don't listen to the old songs that bring you back to the dark place that you used to live in. If you have friends who make you constantly second-guess yourself, maybe you need to find some new friends. You need to consciously think about who you invest your time in, and their impact on the way you view yourself and God's goodness.

Finally, press on! - As Paul stated in Philippians 3:12-14:

[12] Not that I have already attained, or am already perfected; but I press on, that I may lay hold of that for which Christ Jesus has also laid hold of me. [13] Brethren, I do not count myself to have apprehended; but one thing I do, forgetting those things which are behind and reaching forward to those things which are ahead, [14] I press toward the goal for the prize of the upward call of God in Christ Jesus. (NKJV)

Prayer:

Father, I thank you again for the things that you have done in my life these past weeks. I ask that you prepare me to move forward in a way that I can maintain my freedom. I ask you to teach me how to read the Bible in a way that it comes alive to me. I ask that you would teach me to pray and to worship in a more fulfilling way. I ask for grace to spend time with your people, and to love them the way that you love me. And finally, I ask you to help me to make good decisions in my life so I can 'press on'. In Jesus' Name, amen!

30. Thanksgiving

¹¹While He was on the way to Jerusalem, He was passing between Samaria and Galilee. ¹²As He entered a village, ten leprous men who stood at a distance met Him; ¹³and they raised their voices, saying, "Jesus, Master, have mercy on us!" ¹⁴When He saw them, He said to them, "Go and show yourselves to the priests." And as they were going, they were cleansed. ¹⁵Now one of them, when he saw that he had been healed, turned back, glorifying God with a loud voice, ¹⁶and he fell on his face at His feet, giving thanks to Him. And he was a Samaritan.¹⁷Then Jesus answered and said, "Were there not ten cleansed? But the nine—where are they? ¹⁸Was no one found who returned to give glory to God, except this foreigner?" ¹⁹And He said to him, "Stand up and go; your faith has made you well." Luke 17:11-19 (NASB)

This chapter in Luke gives an insight into the levels of healing that we can achieve. In verse fourteen the lepers were all cleansed. The word 'cleansed' means made clean or purified. In essence, they were healed of their leprosy. But in verse nineteen Jesus says the man was made well, or *sozo* in the Greek. That word refers to being saved and made whole. The man who came back to share his gratitude received much more than the others. Their skin was touched, but he was touched by Jesus to the core of his being. There was an intimate exchange between them. Jesus is moved by thanksgiving, and considering all He has done for us, it is an honor to find ways to touch His heart!

Take some time to reflect on the changes that you have experienced during this journey. Write down the things that you are thankful for, and take time to worship the Lord for His unending patience and kindness towards us!

_____

_____

_____

_____

_____

_____

_____

_____

_____

_____

_____

_____

_____

_____

_____

_____

_____

_____

_____

_____

_____

_____

_____

_____

31. Vision

On Day 1 we looked at both Esther and Joseph, who spent significant amounts of time being purified in preparation for their purpose. You have set aside time for spiritual cleansing and purification, as well, and now you are at the end of that process. As we come to a close, it would be fitting for you to ask the Lord to close all of the areas that you have opened up and examined, and to seal them tightly in His love. Next, I encourage you to seek out the joyful areas of your relationship with God. I hope that you will continue to seek out who He says you are, based on the finished work of Jesus, and endeavor to live according to that knowledge. You are wholly and completely loved by your Father, God, and He will work all things together for your good, and for His purposes for you. Jeremiah 29:11 says:

11 'For I know the plans that I have for you,' declares the LORD, 'plans for welfare and not for calamity to give you a future and a hope.' (NASB)

Take time today to ask Him to show you where He would like to take you next. Listen for His guidance about how to stay strong and any advice He might give you. Ask Him to give you vision, new focus, as you move on to the next thing. Then write it all down, as an act of faith and trust. Habakkuk 2:2-3 says:

Then the LORD answered me and said, "Record the vision and inscribe *it* on tablets, that the one who reads it may run. 3 "For the vision is yet for the appointed time; it hastens toward the goal and it will not fail. Though it tarries, wait for it; for it will certainly come, it will not delay. (NASB)

Prayer:

Father, as I wind down this experience, I ask that you would close any doors in my soul that have been opened. Please seal them tightly in your love, and help me to walk in the new truths that I have discovered. I ask that you would show me what you would like for me to focus on next. Please give me new vision for the future, and lead me in a close and personal way. I ask that you would fill my next steps with joy and hope, and show me more about how you see me. Thank you! I love you! In Jesus' Name, amen!

What is next?

_____

_____

_____

_____

_____

_____

_____

_____

_____

_____

_____

_____